A Short Introduction to

User Interface Prototyping

(For Software Development Projects)

By C.W. OH et al

Table of Content

1. Introduction: Why User Interface Prototyping?

User interface prototyping gives a very visual way, and possibly a colorful way, to software development projects. In our view, having and not having user interface prototyping are synonymous to the comparison between MS-DOS (i.e. text-based command prompt oriented) and Apple's Macintosh (i.e. visually oriented with graphical user interface.)

We are strong advocates for the use of user interface prototyping methods in software development projects. Why? It is because user interface prototyping is an excellent method that is capable of providing a common vision and idea of how the final software will look like visually and its behaviors, to all the people involved in the software development projects, and who may come from different backgrounds. As the saying goes, "A picture is worth a thousand words."

We believe that user interface prototyping gives a good discussion reference for the people developing the software and the people that will use the software. This is where both parties can agree on the visuals and behaviors of the eventual software, without waiting for the software product to be developed. User Interface prototyping also gives a mechanism for these two groups of people to agree on the software requirements, especially when the requirements are vague, not defined, and/or implied.

By adopting the user interface prototyping process, it puts the owners and the end-user into the serious thought of how they want the eventual software will look and behave and how it can help in their business process.

We also believe that by adopting and incorporating user interface prototyping early into the software project schedule, and iterating it until the eventual software is available for demonstration, it gives opportunities for the end-user to feedback their preferences and expectations of the eventual software. It will also give the development team to have a constant communication channel with the end-users and will greatly reduces the possibility of the end-user of coming back at the end of the software development to claim, "... what is this? This is not what I want! What I want is ...!" and the disagreement continues.

In this book, we will introduce to you the user interface prototyping process, low fidelity and high fidelity user interface prototypes, and we will also show an example of user interface prototyping, i.e. Point-of-Sale system.

2. User Interface Prototyping Process

The flow-chart diagram below (Diagram 2-A) shows a typical user interface prototyping process.

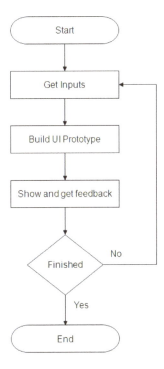

Figure 1: User Interface Prototyping Process

The user interface prototyping process is designed to be iterative. This iterative process allows all participants to come out with ideas, experimenting with different colors, layouts and graphics and make changes. For every each iteration, new needs and ideas are incorporated into the user interface prototype and changes are made. Until when everyone agrees with the look and feel of the prototype, the user interface prototype is then finalized and agreed.

The diagram below (Diagram 2-B) shows a simplified view of the number of changes and the number of confirmations of a typical user interface prototyping process. It is expected that there will be changes at the start. These changes will reduce over time as the prototype undergoes iterations of feedbacks and corrections. Correspondingly, the number of confirmations will increase, until no further change is requested.

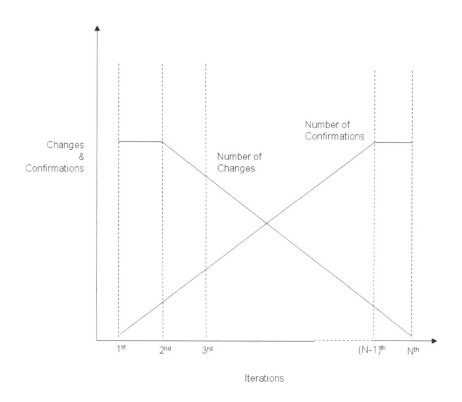

Figure 2: Prototyping Iterations versus Changes and Confirmations

However, there is also catch to this iterative process, i.e. "How many iterations?" In concept, it can go forever, i.e. nth iteration, but this will defeat the purpose of adopting user interface prototyping in software development projects. While there is a no definite answer but there are rule-of-thumbs that we can follow and adapt at the end of each iteration.

- What are the objectives for this iteration?
- What needs to be changed?
- What is to be kept?
- What needs to be added?
- Anything else?

And where time and cost are the limits, it might be necessary to limit the number of iterations and have specific objectives for the prototyping process and at each iteration. In addition, it is also a good idea to have specific exit conditions.

3. Low Fidelity User Interface Prototyping

Most user interface on computer screens and smart phones can be modeled using simple of tools such as paper, pencils, pens, sticky notes, and flip charts. The advantage of using these tools is its simplicity and low-cost. They can be produced easily, and any changes can be corrected and shown almost immediately. Its ability for a fast turnaround time to incorporate any modifications, allows the end-user's thoughts and expectations to be captured at that point, minimizing differences between the end-user and the people developing the software.

While low-fidelity user interface prototyping in its simple printed on paper form does not give the ability for interaction, this can be enhanced to incorporate simple interaction to show and capture the behavior of the eventual software, i.e. through the use of sticky notes, flip charts, story-boarding and the 'Human Computer' methods. We have to bear in mind that the main focus that we want to achieve is more on the design of the user-interface design than the technology used.

The following sections will discuss how we can use these different methods of low fidelity user interface prototyping.

3.1. Story Boarding

A storyboard defined here is a user interface flow diagram consisting of boxes depicting the screens that are connected together by arrows showing the path and the actions needed to proceed to the next screens.

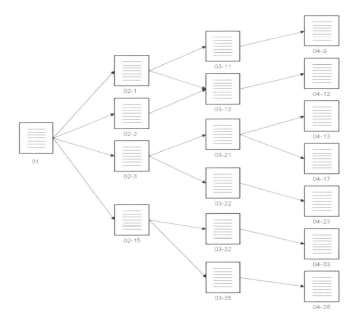

Figure 3: Storyboard

The purpose of storyboard essentially is to show the high level picture of the software, such that anyone that sees the storyboard can quickly understand how the software will work or behave. In addition, it also used to define the role of the software and how the software can achieve business objectives.

3.2. Using Paper and Pencil

In its simplest form, the screens on the computer and smart phones can be represented by drawing the screen on a piece of paper using a pencil. These simple hand drawn screens can be further elaborated to include colors, using color pencils or color pens.

Figure 4: Paper Prototype Using a Pencil

Figure 5: Paper Prototype in Color

And with every new piece of paper, the individual screens are drawn. These drawings are then checked with the end-user for feedback. Changes are made, rejected papers are thrown away and the screens are re-drawn on to new pieces of paper.

The down side of this is that it can only give a static view of the user interface. The subsequent sections will show us how we can improve further to give simple 'manual' dynamic contents to our hand-drawn screens.

3.3. Using Sticky Notes

Sticky notes are indispensible tool in user interface prototyping. It is most capable in giving screen behavior to the paper prototype mentioned in the earlier section.

Figure 6: Sticky Notes

Sticky notes can be used for show screen changes when a user command is received from the user-user, e.g. drop down menus, tabs navigations, check boxes, etc.

The two diagrams below (Diagram 3.3B and Diagram 3.3C) illustrate a simple usage showing the possible selections for a combo box when filling up an account sign-up form.

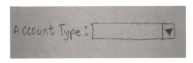

Figure 7: Combo Box for Account Selection

Figure 8: Sticky Note Displays the Selection Available

3.4. Using Flip Charts

Flip charts move the interactivity of low fidelity user interface prototyping up one more notch. While sticky notes show behavior on a particular screen, a flip chart gives screen flows behavior. The diagram below (Diagram 3.4A) shows an example to a flip chart.

Figure 9: Flip Chart with Papers and Sticky Notes

Here, screens that were drawn on paper are complied into a flip chart such that when the page is flipped, the next screen is presented. The first or second pages of the flip chart generally should display the first screen and this is followed by the subsequent screens. The positions of the pages are sorted to reduce the number of flips.

Depending on the flow of the user interface, there can be more than one possible next screen, and to reduce the time finding and flipping to the next screen, we will generally number all the screens and put a go to page number on each button that leads to another page. So when we 'click', we can flip directly to that page, without flipping through the whole flip chart to search for d that particular page.

When the flip chart is used together with screen drawings and sticky notes, the screens, the screen behavior and the screen flow behavior can be modeled and put to the test.

3.5.   The Human Computer

The Human Computer is the accumulation of low fidelity user interface prototyping. In simple terms, this is a walkthrough of the screens and the behavior of the prototype, with the Human Computer acting as the computer running the application. The whole set for this requires at least two persons, a table with two chairs and the low fidelity prototypes and tools mentioned earlier.

The diagram below (Diagram 3.5A) shows a typical setup.

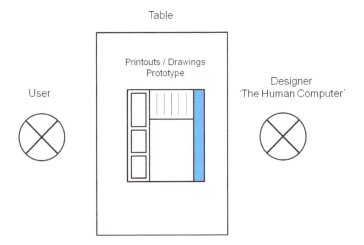

Figure 10: The Human Computer versus User

From the diagram above, we have:

- The Designer or 'The Human Computer, will represent the computer processing the commands and updating the screens on the table, emulating the behavior of the software application.
- The Table will represent the screen showing the paper prototypes which are updated by 'The Human Computer' when command is received from the User.
- The User will be the candidate that will interact with 'The Human Computer' through the Table. The user 'clicks' on the screen, and

It is essential that some preparation work should have already been done before the 'running the application', e.g. the screens prototype and the behavior of the system. And to make the session a better, both parties need to describe to each other their actions. Where required, the Designer will do quick corrections to the drawings, if changes need to be done.

The session can be video recorded so that any feedbacks can be recorded and incorporated into the final system.

3.6. Other Low Fidelity Tools

While we have covered the use of pencils, color pencils, paper, sticky notes to create low fidelity user interface prototypes, we go further to introduce user interface stencil to help in drawing screens, and components. The diagram below (Diagram 3.6A) shows an example of the user interface stencil.

Figure 11: User Interface Stencil

There are also other ways of creating such prototypes, i.e. through the use of PowerPoint, Visio, or any other similar software to draw the screens and screen components. Once drawn, the screens are printed using the printers (with colors). Alternatively, these drawings can be presented over big screens.

These methods are excellent when you have people that are very good at drawing diagrams using such software. The following are some of such tools for creating low fidelity user interface prototypes:

- Microsoft PowerPoint; http://office.microsoft.com/en-001/powerpoint/
- Microsoft Visio; http://office.microsoft.com/en-001/visio/
- Pencil; http://pencil.evolus.vn/
- Balsamiq; http://balsamiq.com/

4. High Fidelity User Interface Prototyping

Moving up the difficulty chart, we can use software programs to draw the screens and we add interactions to our prototype. High fidelity approach brings us closer to the final system user interface and allows realistic user interactions, e.g. mouse, keyboard, navigation between screens, and screen behaviors.

There are numerous tools and resources available to produce high fidelity prototypes, but for our discussion, we will introduce HTML, Microsoft Visual Studio Express, and Java – NetBeans. The following sections will discuss how we can use these tools for high fidelity user interface prototyping.

A point to note here when creating high fidelity user interface prototype is to focus on the appearance and interactions and not how the codes are structured and the libraries are designed. This will be especially true when the tools used are the same for developing the final product.

4.1. Using HTML

If the final system is for the web, it makes sense that we build our prototype in its natural environment. In this approach, HTML pages are created as the prototype. The menus, hyperlinks and other screen elements will represent the different interactions available.

The prototype can be adapted to the width of the browser window and the different widths of different screens.

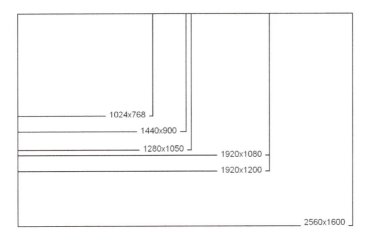

Figure 12: Sample of Different Screen Sizes

When it is hosted on the internet, the prototype can be easily accessed and viewed, as long as there is internet connectivity.

The resources available on-line on 'how-to' create web pages are huge, and your creativity is your limit. There are numerous tools and methods available to build HTML prototypes depending on the complexity of the prototypes. The tools used can also include tools that will be selected and used to build the final product, e.g. Adobe Dreamweaver, Notepad++, and Coffeecup. And with the introduction of HTML5 with CSS, it makes it even simpler to create interactive and exciting HTML pages.

The following are some of our recommended resources for prototyping using HTML:

- HTML online resource; http://www.w3schools.com/html/
- Adobe Dreamweaver, http://www.adobe.com/
- Notepad ++, http://notepad-plus-plus.org/
- CoffeeCup, http://www.coffeecup.com/
- Netbeans, https://netbeans.org/
- Microsoft Visual Studio, http://www.visualstudio.com/
- Bootstrap, http://getbootstrap.com/
- Foundation, http://foundation.zurb.com/

For example, the diagram below (Diagram 4.1B) shows a simple HTML UI prototype using Notepad++, focusing on the buttons, layout and display. The mathematical function was not implemented for this prototype.

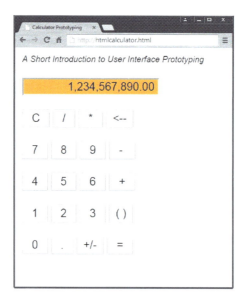

Figure 13: HTML with Calculator User Interface Prototype

4.2. Using Microsoft Visual Studio

Microsoft Visual Studio is a well known IDE to many developers developing programs on Microsoft Windows. The latest iteration of the Visual Studio at the time of this writing is Visual Studio 2013. It comes is several editions, i.e. Professional, Premium, Ultimate, Test Professional and Community. The Community edition is the free version offered by Microsoft.

More information about Microsoft Visual Studio can be found that its website, http://www.visualstudio.com/.

We general recommend the use of Visual Basic or Visual C# in Microsoft Visual Studio because of the advantages that we see in Visual Studio for UI prototyping, i.e.:

- Quick in creating screen/forms,
- Quick 'Drag and Drop' from toolbox to form,
- Quick setup for forms navigations,
- Quick learning curve on the 'Object.Properties' when more functionalities are required in the prototype.

And because the above mentioned actions above can be done relatively with ease, a simple calculator UI prototype can be completed within 10 minutes.

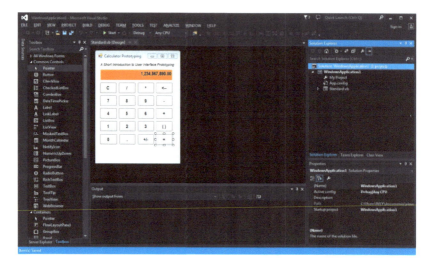

Figure 14: Microsoft Visual Studio Integrated Development Environment with Calculator User Interface Prototype

4.3. Using Java - NetBeans

Netbeans provides a similar IDE experience as Microsoft's Visual Studio, but in Java development environment. We also like the use of NetBeans when creating UI prototype because of its 'Drag and Drop' from the toolbox functionality. This enables us to be able to create and amend screens quickly without needing to worry about the underlining codes.

And because of this, we were able to also create a simple calculator UI prototype within 10 minutes. The diagram below (Diagram 4.3A) shows this working.

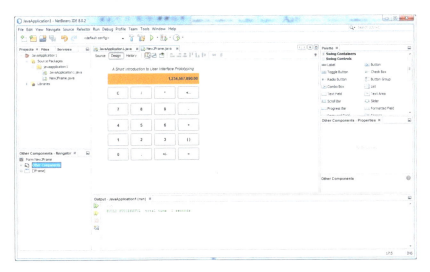

Figure 15: NetBeans Integrated Development Environment with Calculator User Interface Prototype

4.4. Other High Fidelity Tools

So far we have only introduced to you three tools for high fidelity prototyping that we have used. However these are not the only tools available in the market. The following are some of our recommended tools:

- Bootstrap; http://getbootstrap.com/
- Axure; http://www.axure.com/
- GUI Design Studio; http://www.carettasoftware.com/guidesignstudio/
- Adobe Flash Professional CC; http://www.adobe.com/products/flash.html

5. Beyond User Interface Prototyping

While User Interface Prototyping, the process and activities, is a colorful and visually exciting exercise which gives immense satisfaction to us. We are encouraged by the use of user interface prototyping in supporting software projects, and we believe it can contribute to a good completion to software development projects and with the end-users continue to use the delivered system after delivery.

While it is neither an exotic method nor a 'silver bullet' solution to the perils of software development projects, it gives visibility and confidence to all stakeholders throughout the duration of the development of the software and until the final system is delivered. In that sense, it supports the software development projects in confirming the requirements, guides the design and development, and sets expectations duration acceptance testing and the eventual use of the final system.

And moving up a notch further, we prototype and model other segments of the software projects, e.g.

- Usability – where we further demonstrate that the user interface and accessibility are intuitive and complement the human behaviors and responses,
- Capacity Sizing and Performance – where we demonstrate that the system is capable of performing at various (high) data loads and (high) processing performance,
- Business processes – where we prototype or model that business processes and how any changes improves the business process (optimization).

And by prototyping and modeling the different segments where possible, we reduce uncertainty and improve the survivability of the software projects.

6. Exercise: Prototyping a Point-of-Sale System

We now introduce to you a simple working exercise of prototyping a Point-of-Sale (POS) system user interface for a grocery store.

We start by defining some simple the requirements for our point-of-sale system. We will then use Microsoft PowerPoint as a tool to create the screens of our low fidelity prototype of the point-of-sale system.

We will attempt to showcase the progression of the prototype over three iterations of user interface prototyping, with the defined objectives for each of the iterations.

- Iteration #1:
    - To define the major screens required for the point-of-sale system user interface.
    - To define the navigation structure between the screens.
    - To define the screens layouts.

- Iteration #2:
    - To define screens details (simple graphics only).
    - To describe the some of the main transaction operations.

- Iteration #3:
    - To refine the screens details with colors.

Once the prototype is completed, we will table the requirements and trace these requirements to the elements of the prototype to showcase and proof the fulfillment of the requirements, i.e. Traceability Matrix.

6.1 Our Initial Requirements

1. The system shall maintain a database of items that are for sale in the grocery store.

2. The user shall be able select the items from the database and add them into the purchase item list.

3. The purchase item list shall display the item purchased, the unit price of the item, the quantity purchased, and the sub-total for the item.

4. The system shall be able to show the total price of all items purchased.

5. The system shall have number pad to enter the price, quantity, or the item unique ID of the items to be purchased.

6. The system shall have an end-of-day collection summary function.

7. The system shall have a sign-off and sign-on security function.

6.2   User Interface Prototype Iteration #1

With our understanding of the initial requirements, we first define the screens for our point-of-sale system and create a storyboard for the screen navigations.

- Sign-in screen
  This screen receives access code for signing into the Point-of-Sale system. A valid access code will be required to access the system.

- Main screen
  This is the main screen of main of the point of sale system, where point-of-sale transactions are entered.

- Maintain item screen
  This is the screen where items that are for sale in the grocery shop are maintained. New items are added, out-of-stock items removed, and existing items updated (if needed). This is also the place where discounts and offers are added into the system also. This screen is access through the Manager function.

- Maintain staff screen
  This screen maintains staff records accessing the point-of-sale system. This is where security access number is allocated to staff to access into the Point-of-Sale system. This screen is access through the Manager function.

- End-of-Day screen
  This screen performs the end-of-day operation. It shall show the total amount monies registered by the system. This amount must tally with the cash and discount coupons in the cash drawer.

The following diagram (Diagram Ex-1-1) defines the storyboard.

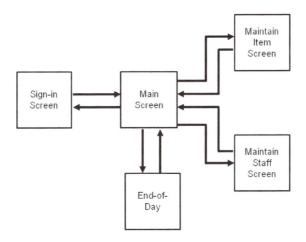

Figure 16: Storyboard for Our Point-of-Sale System

Next, we define the layout of the major areas for our point-of-sale system user interfaces for all the screens, i.e. Sign-in screen, Main screen, Maintain Item screen and Maintain Staff screen. The following diagrams (Diagram Ex-1-2, Diagram Ex-1-3, Diagram Ex-1-4, Diagram Ex-1-5 and Diagram Ex-1-6) define the major areas for all the four screens for our point-of-sale user interface prototype.

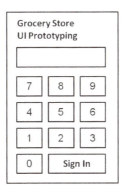

Figure 17: Sign-in Screen

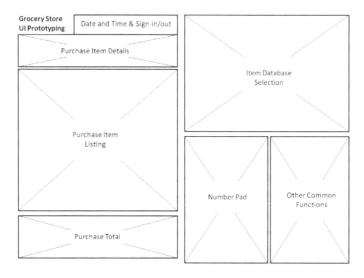

Figure 18: Major Areas for Main Screen

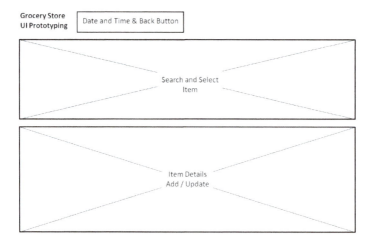

Figure 19: Major Areas for Maintain Item Screen

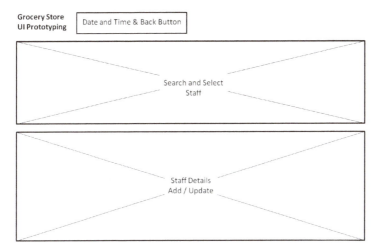

Figure 20: Major Areas for Maintain Staff Screen

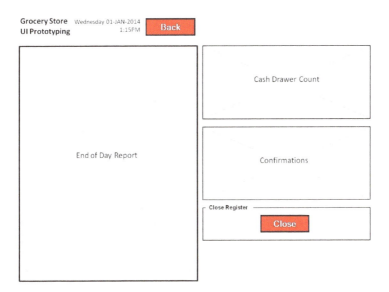

Figure 21: Major Areas for End-of-Day Screen

B. User Interface Prototype Iteration #2

Next we add details to the major areas of the screens defined during iteration #1. The following diagrams (Diagram Ex-1-6, Diagram Ex-1-7, Diagram Ex-1-8 and Diagram Ex-1-9) show the respective screen mentioned in iteration #1 with more details. The major operations are also described.

Sign-in Screen operation

- User enters unique access code number and press 'Sign in' button.

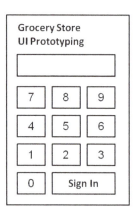

Figure 22: Sign-in Screen with Details

Main Screen operations *(not exhaustive)*

- Press 'New Transaction' to start.

- To enter item(s) into the purchasing list:
  i. Press Items from the item database, or
  ii. Press 'No Scan' followed by the product number on the product and press 'Enter'
  iii. If the is no more item to enter, press 'Total' to finalize the amount payable.
  iv. Press payment to register the amount received.

- To maintain item database or staff access, press 'Manager Function'.

- To perform end-of-day or end-of-shift and collection summary function, press 'Manager Function'.

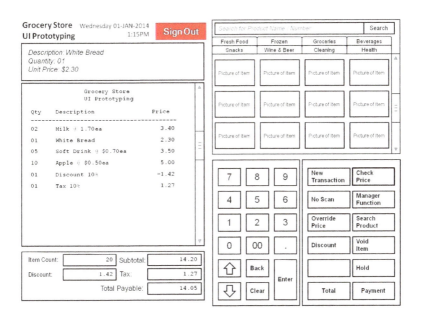

Figure 23: Main Screen with Details

Manager Function Screen Operation

- Press 'Maintain Item Database' to manage items for sale in the grocery store.

- Press 'Maintain Staff Database' to manage staff access code.

Figure 24: Manager Functions

Maintain Item Screen Operation (not exhaustive)

- To add new item, Press 'New' and enter the product details. Press 'Update' to save the product details.

- To update an existing product, staff needs to search for the product first.

- To search for an existing product, enter the product name or number and press 'Search'. Short listed records will be displayed in the record(s) found list.

- To update the product in the record(s) found list, press 'Select' on the selected row. The selected product details will be presented in the product details section. Click 'Edit', and update the fields. Press 'Update' to save the product details.

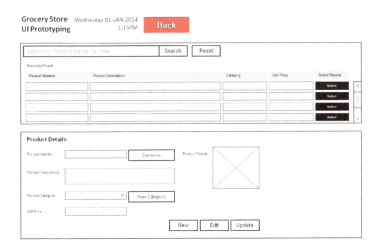

Figure 25: Maintain Item Screen with Details

Maintain Staff Screen Operation (not exhaustive)

- To add new staff, Press 'New' and enter the staff details. Press 'Update' to save the staff details.

- To update an existing staff, supervisor needs to search for the staff first.

- To search for an existing staff, enter the product name or number and press 'Search'. Short listed records will be displayed in the record(s) found list.

- To update the staff in the record(s) found list, press 'Select' on the selected row. The selected staff details will be presented in the product details section. Click 'Edit', and update the fields. Press 'Update' to save the product details.

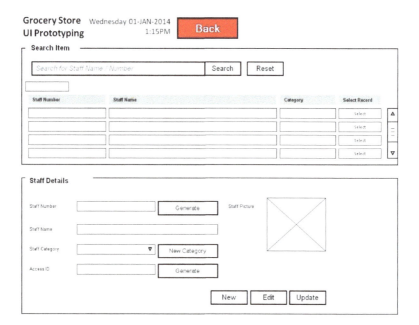

Figure 26: Maintain Staff Screen with Details

End of Day Operation (not exhaustive)

- Count the cash amount in the cash drawer, enter the cash value and click the check box.

- Count the cheque amount in the cash drawer, enter the cheque value and click the check box.

- Count the coupon amount in the cash drawer, enter the coupon value and click the check box.

- Cashier enters ID and press 'Confirm'.

- Supervisor double-checks all amounts are correct, enters supervisor ID and press 'Confirm'.

- Supervisor press 'Submit' to submit the data to centralized HQ system.

- Cashier or Supervisor press 'Close' to close the register.

Figure 27: End-of-Day Screen with Details

C. User Interface Prototype Iteration #3

Finally, we do some touch-up of our prototype screens to make it look more presentable.

Figure 28: Sign-in Screen

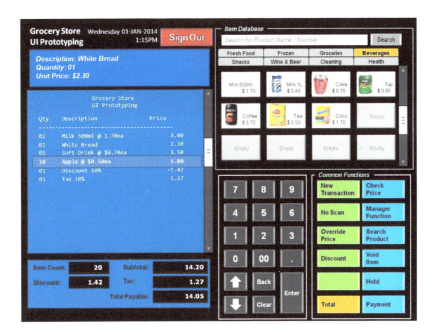

Figure 29: Main Screen

Figure 30: Manager Functions Screen

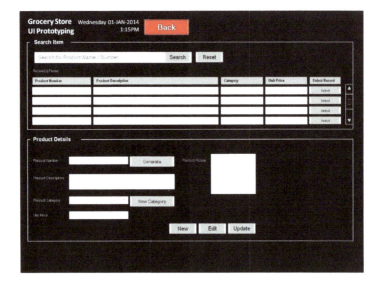

Figure 31: Maintain Item Screen

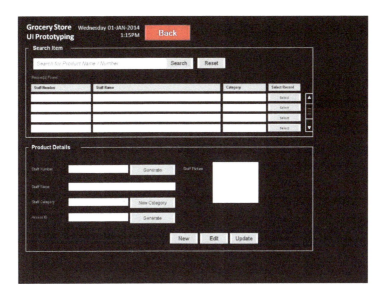

Figure 32: Maintain Staff Screen

Figure 33: End-of-Day Screen

D. Tracing to Requirements

Next we attempt to trace and prove that our point-of-sale user interface prototype is capable to fulfilling all the seven requirements we defined at the start of this user interface prototyping exercise.

Requirement Description (1):

"The system shall maintain a database of items that are for sale in the grocery store."

Evidence (1):

(a) In the main screen, the cashier can search for item in the database. Items that are for sale by the store will be displayed.

(b) In the maintain item screen, new items can be added and existing items can be updated.

Requirement Description (2):

"The user shall be able select the items from the database and add them into the purchase item list."

Evidence (2):

(a) In the main screen, the cashier can search for item in the database. Items that are for sale by the store will be displayed.

Requirement Description (3):

*"The purchase item list shall display
the item purchased, the unit price of
the item, the quantity purchased, and
the sub-total for the item."*

Evidence (3):

(a) In the main screen, shows

- Items purchased,

- Unit price for the items,

- Quantity of items, and

- Sub-total of the items

Requirement Description (4):

"The system shall be able to show the
total price of all items purchased."

Evidence (4):

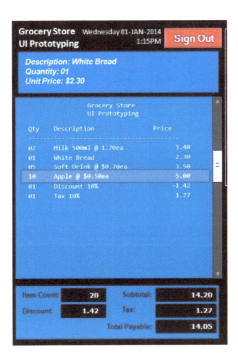

(a) In the main screen, the total price of all items purchased is shown.

Requirement Description (5):

"The system shall have number pad to enter the price, quantity, or the item unique ID of the items to be purchased."

Evidence (5)

(a) In the main screen, the number pad is available for the cashier to enter the price, quantity, or the item unique ID of the items to be purchased.

Requirement (6):

"The system shall have an end-of-day collection summary function."

Evidence (6):

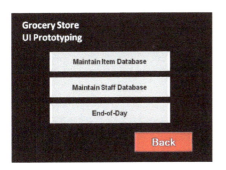

(a) In the Manager Function with go to End-of-Day function.

(b) In the End-of-Day screen, end of day collection summary shown.

Requirement (7):

"The system shall have a sign-off and
sign-on security function."

Evidence (7):

(a) In the sign-in screen, the
cashier enters access
code to access the
point-of-sale system.

(b) In the main screen, Sign-
out button for the
cashier to sign-out of
the system.

In Summary

Using the user interface prototype, we were able to provide evidences and proof that all the seven requirements are met. This gives us immediate confidence that if the eventual point-of-sale system development follows the prototype, we can then be confident that the eventual system will also meet all these seven requirements.

About the Authors

C.W. OH and team are advocates for good user interface designs, particularly in the support of software development projects. They believe user interface prototyping gives direction and guides the software development, and helps to manage the different stakeholders of the software projects.

OH worked as a project manager and had previously worked in project teams that delivered software systems to critical installations for private and government entities. He can be reached at c.w.oh.et.al@gmail.com.

www.ingramcontent.com/pod-product-compliance
Lightning Source LLC
LaVergne TN
LVHW012316070326

832902LV00001BA/21